A Present f

Story by Jackie Tid

Photography by Lindsay E

Rigby®

A Harcourt Achieve Imprint

www.Rigby.com

1-800-531-5015

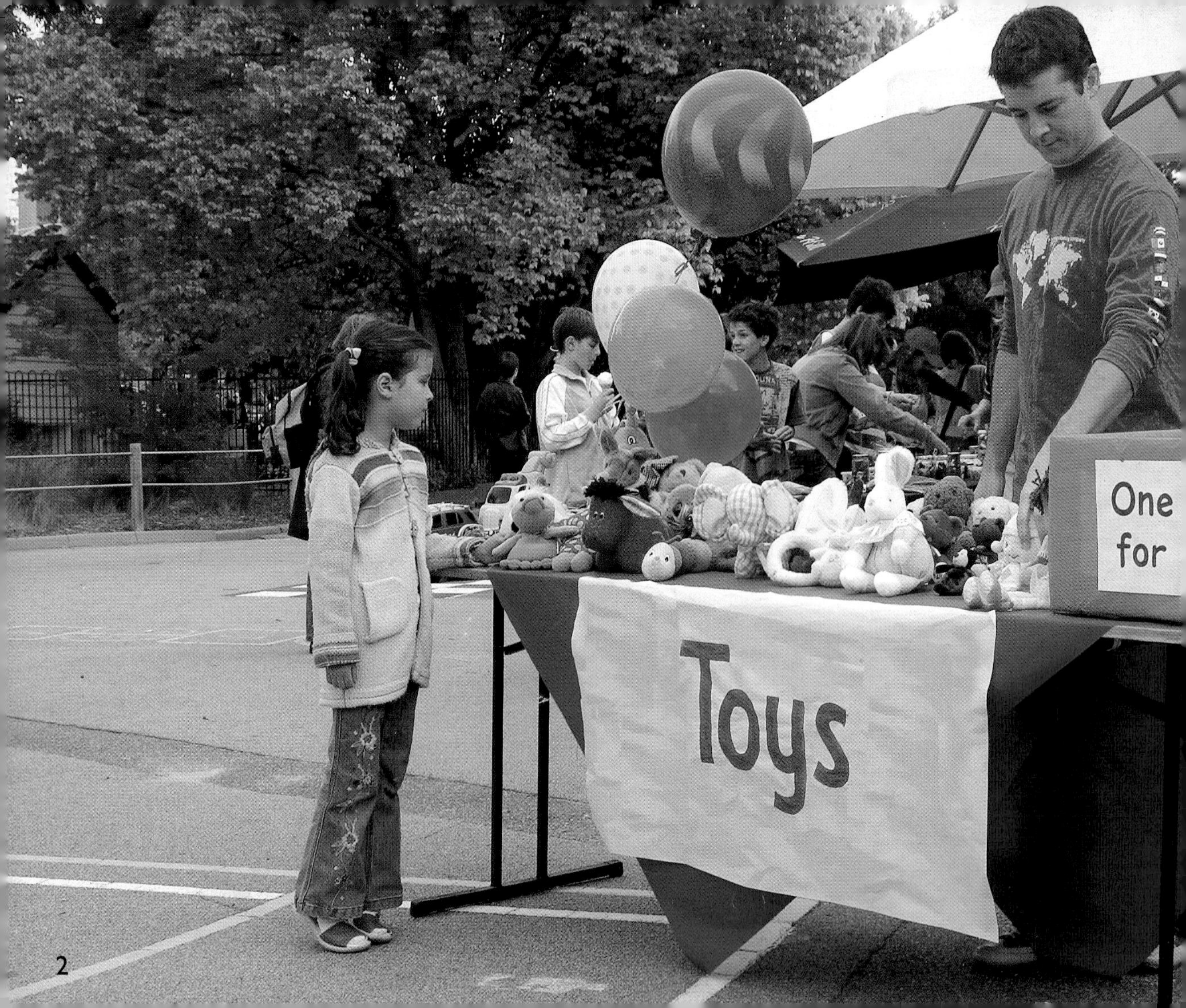
One
for
Toys

Bella is looking

for a toy.

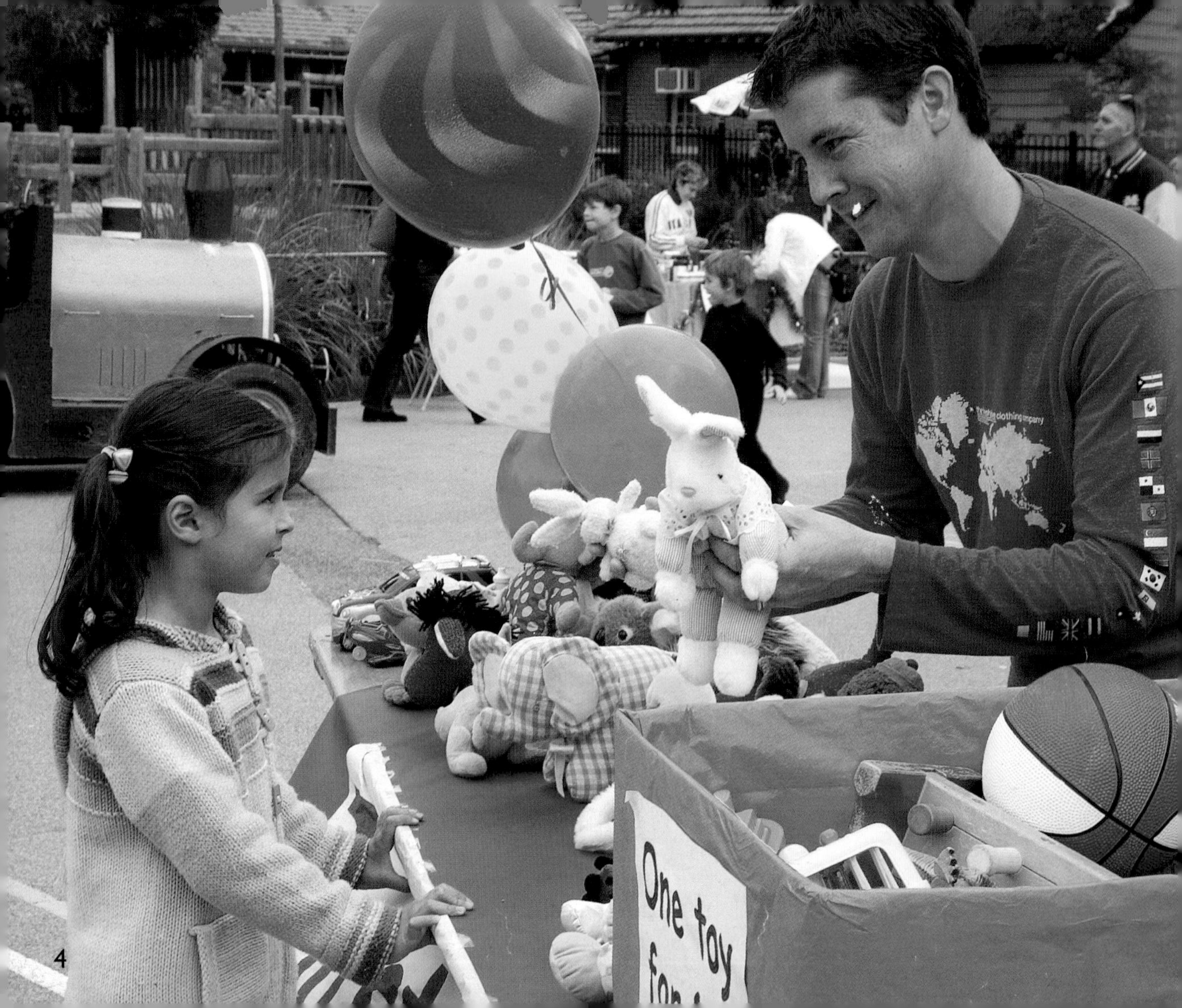
One toy

"Here are rabbits,"
said the man.

"No, thank you," said Bella.

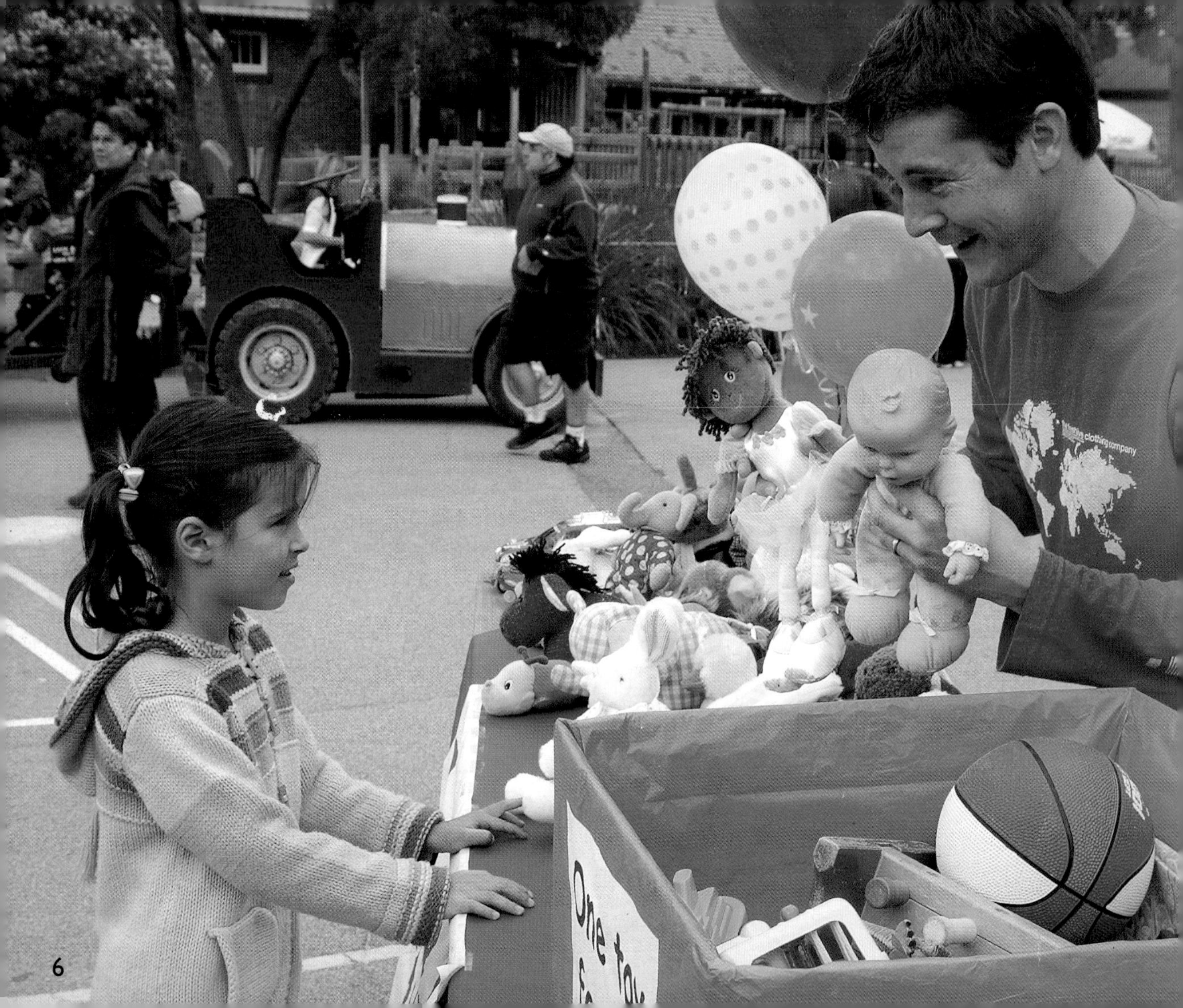
clothing company
One

"Here are dolls,"

said the man.

"No, thank you," said Bella.

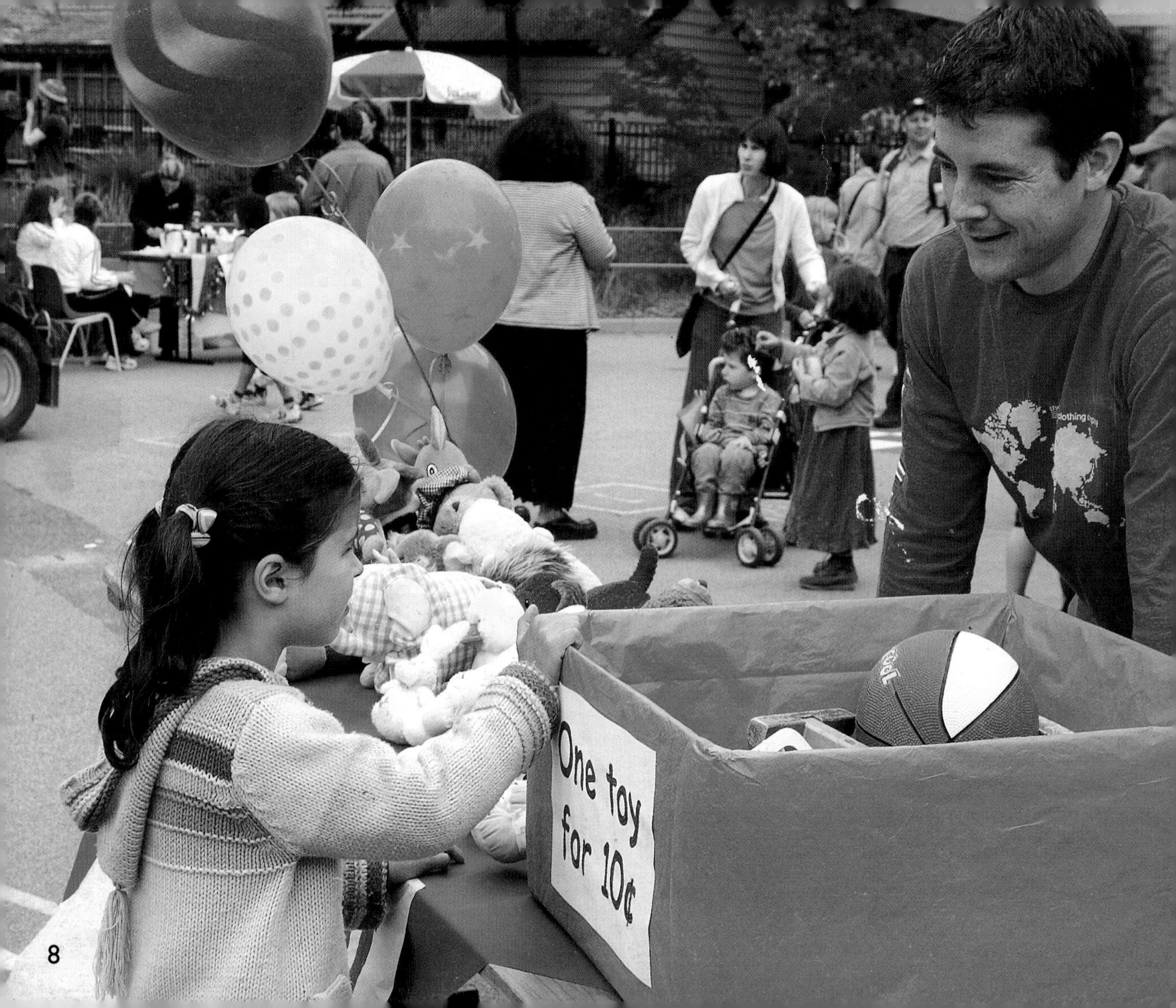
One toy
for 10¢

Bella looked at the big box.

"Can I look in here?"

said Bella.

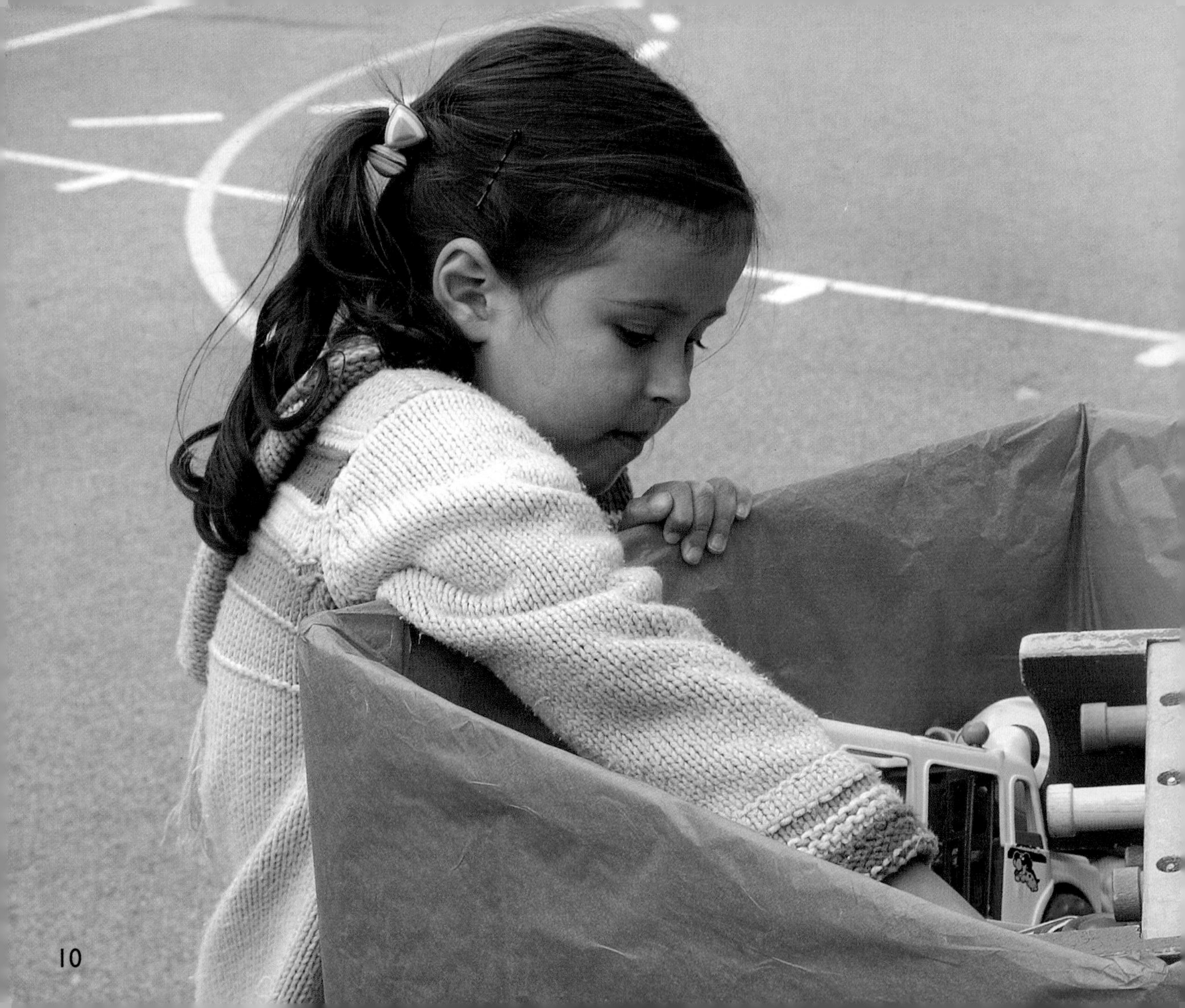

Bella looked and looked

in the big box.

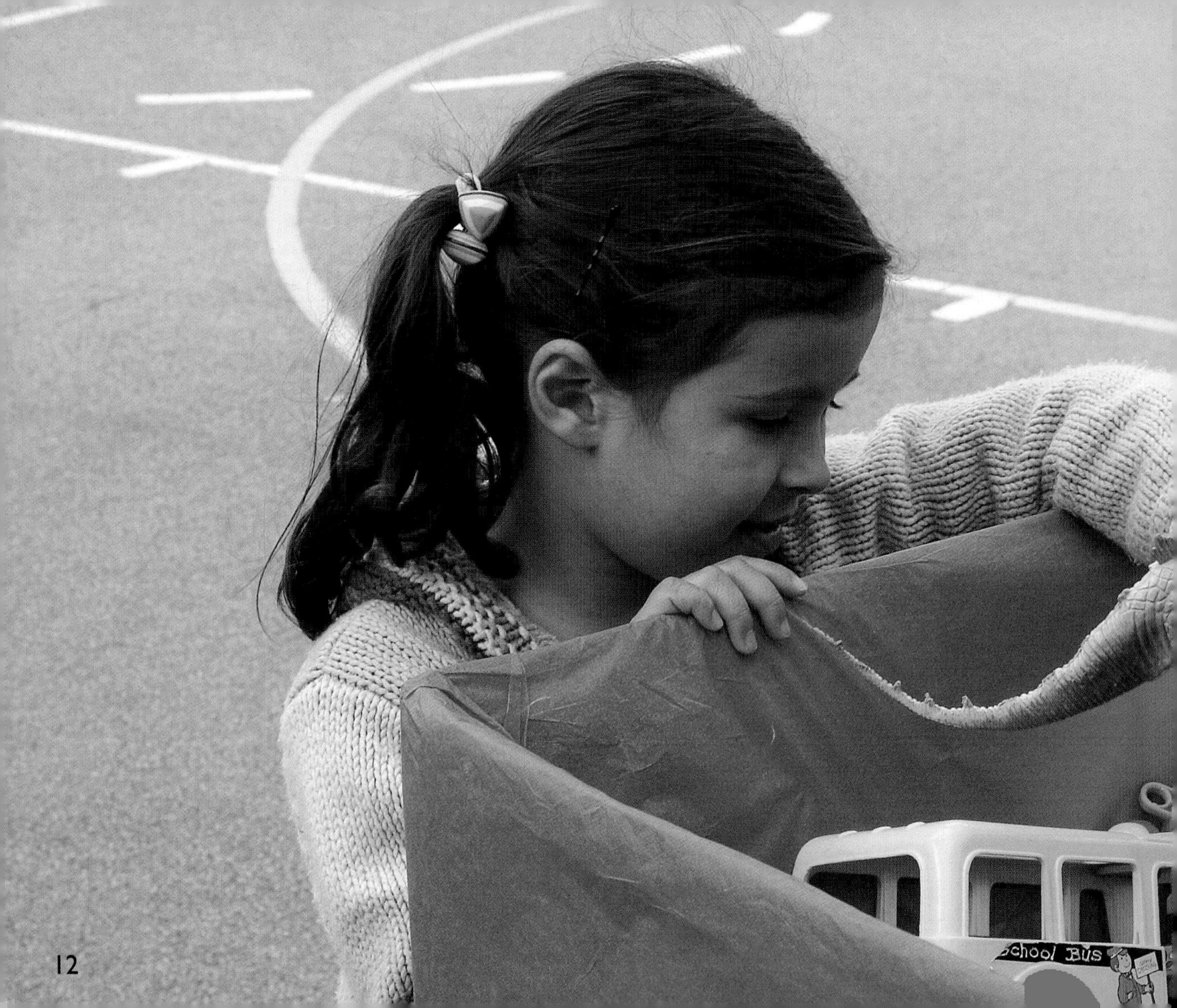
School Bus

"Oh!" said Bella.

"Here is a dinosaur!"

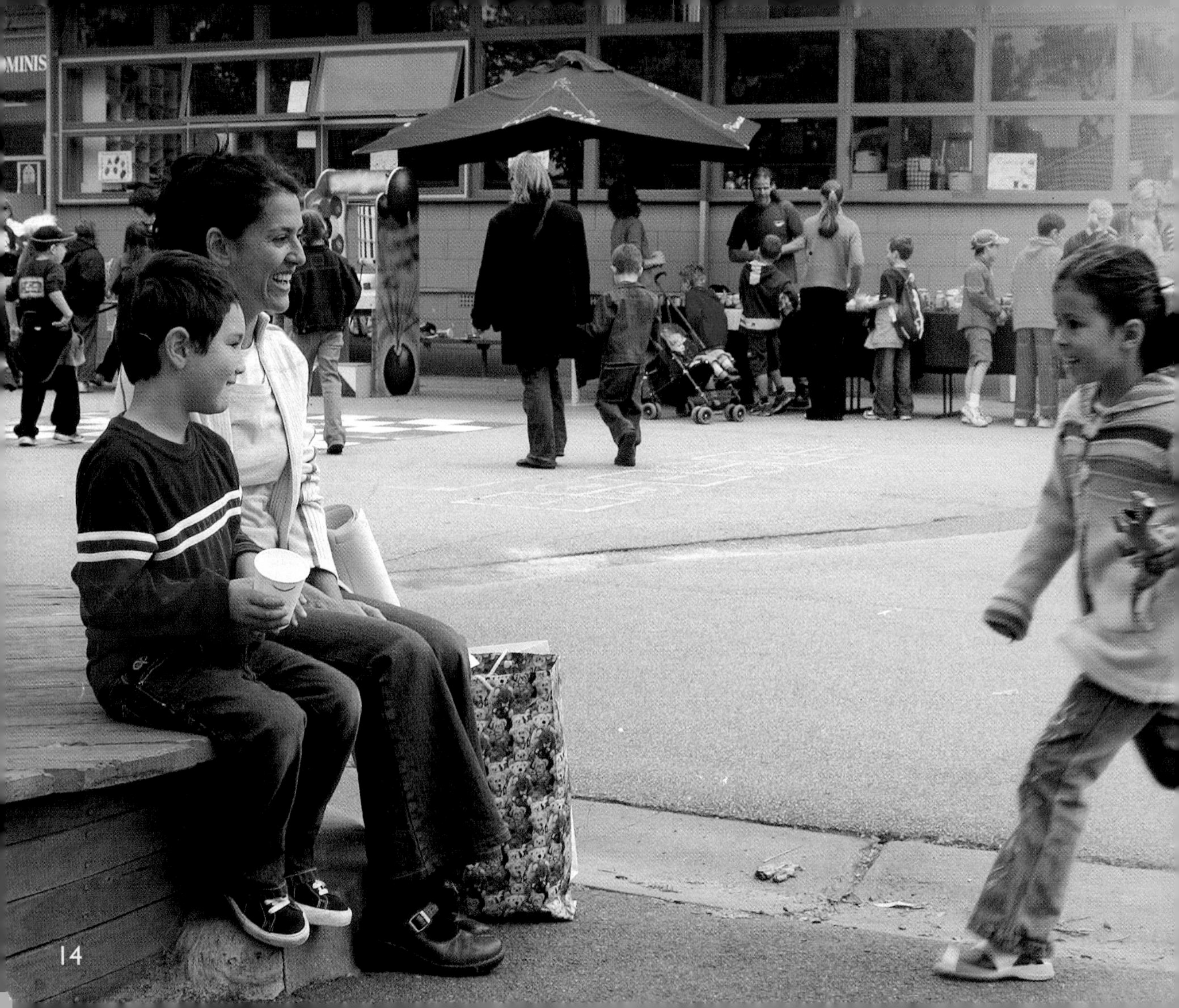
MINIS

Bella ran to Mom and Karl.

"Karl! Karl!" said Bella.

"Here is a dinosaur for you."

"A dinosaur for me!" said Karl.

"Thank you, Bella."